Contents

AF085374

Tru Paraha
in my darkling universe

Modi Deng
安慰 *(an wei)*

Foreword

The poets whose work is brought together in *AUP New Poets 8* all write with an intoxicating sense of the world's beauty, its depth and distances. They write with an awareness, too, of the depths and distances that can be found within relationships and within the self. All three poets are concerned with memory and its traces, with artistry and the forms it can take, with the natural world at its most infinitesimal and at its most vast. You will encounter in these poems lilting bees and unidentifiable birds, long-division problems and continental cornflakes, stars and asterisks, risks and trespasses, impulse buys and neon zines, orchards full of āporo, a motel's net curtains, sharded ephemera, beautiful handwriting, Scooby Doo, a farmer's headache, Cleopatra's vulva, thirty-six ice plants, missing letters, quite a lot of helium and even more glitter.

In 'hopscotch' Lily Holloway unclips her skull 'like a sistema lunch-box' and stick insects scuttle out 'as if it is double-time'. Her collection, 'a child in that alcove', gives a good sense of how rich her inner life is, how teeming her mind, and how lively her observations as she watches children playing hopscotch, ducklings tumbing behind a mother duck in the surf, Facebook advertising Velma Dinkley t-shirts and a helium balloon in the shape of an S floating free as a box kite over the harbour. Full of the ordinarily extraordinary events that make up everyday life, Holloway's collection has a darker undercurrent to it than is immediately apparent. Her body 'a monument / to never / forgetting', her poems, too, are shaped by a past that makes itself known to the reader through shadows, repetitions, metaphors, questions, erasures, echoes and a controlled use of form. Her approach to form is inventive – free verse allows spaces to open up on the page or to close the gaps between sentences; the different parts of the body are accounted for in an itemised and annotated list; layout controls pace, as 'moirai' for instance slows down to one word in a line then speeds up into a breathless unspooling; 'a lulling / it's stratified, you know' contains its content within boxy lines even as words fall, hyphenated, down the page. 'return again' resembles a deconstructed sestina, each stanza numbered with six entries that could be notes towards a longer poem or details cut loose from a narrative. The sixth numbered point in every stanza is the same – the instruction 'return again', which might be read as self-reflexive but suggests, too, the way memories return and structure a life. Many images recur again and again in one poem after another – bees, a fence, a Four Square carpark, the sea and its tides and rock pools, insects, trolleys, concrete – and gather resonance with their reappearances. 'my twenty-second year / flickers like the same two seconds / of a deep river, over and over', she writes in 'i am desired', and the flickering light, the underwater panic from this and other lines from other poems illuminates the whole collection with its dazzle and dread, its intermittent and ongoing significance. Questions remain, for the poet and for the reader – 'What is the link between event and after-effect?' she asks in 'Is any of this relevant?' – but the collection as a whole feels very resolved. These are poems full of resilience, tenderness and delight.

Tru Paraha takes formal inventiveness even further in her collection of poems, which spins out across the pages collapsing words within words, worlds within worlds. As a choreographer, Paraha describes her work as extending 'towards performance that shines black at itself', and this same reflective intent illuminates her poetry as well. Her opening poem 'spin' presents us with a 'luminosity rotisserie', allowing accretion and collision, unspooling spaciousness and infinite compression. There is a festive element to the poem with its bouncy castle, the imbibement of helium, its remarks and asides ('how quasar', '[= bwaha]') as well as a sense of the 'aweful' – a vision of a world both awesome and awful, unimaginable in its immensity, its duration, its ultra-violet violence, its invisible maw. The dizzy gravity of the universe becomes, with the crossing out of its 'it', a dizzy gravy; the universe itself is reconceived as an 'Ioverse' (and a tipsy one); te reo is folded into sentences in English mirroring the atomic chemistry – or choreography – the poem celebrates, when 'o te once upon their bodies collide'. These poems are not easily read for narrative or scene-setting and it would be possible to feel a little lost, as a reader, navigating the word-play and unexpected forms of punctuation and layout on the page. Poems appear on the page without even their titles to provide a secure footing for the reader: Paraha explains that she hopes the reader will experience the poem as an artwork might be experienced in a gallery, as an aesthetic experience first before any reaching towards explanatory notes or contextual information. The aim is immersion rather than analysis, experience rather than 'understanding'. The poetry invites the same Romantic response that is expressed within the poetry itself: what more Romantic line could there be than 'love of skyglow   wow ', even if it isn't perhaps quite how Keats would have phrased it? Again and again she looks beyond, ki tua, towards the infinite, to sublime heights and 'wilding frights', expressing a longing to 'die historically'. If a postmodern irony might be detected in her enjoyment of some of these phrases, more important is the way a Romantic sublime is folded into Māori concepts of cosmology; the darkness or 'darknyss' piercing the collection is understood in relation to te pō; the poetry itself is organised in terms of porohita uriuri.

Modi Deng is equally attuned to the Romantic. In one poem she draws on the image of an Aeolian harp, as Coleridge does in his poem 'The Eolian Harp'. Coleridge uses the image of the wind harp, which makes music out of the wind blowing through its strings, as an image for the inspired poet whose poetry comes not from the self but from the world beyond. This is true of Deng's poetry also but she shares equally with Coleridge the idea of conversation, the idea of the Aeolian harp coming from the 'ae-o, ae-o' of an often repeated story, which makes the listener laugh in spades and the story-teller speak with a wobble in their voice. There are all kinds of ways to lose yourself offered in these poems: the same poem invites you to 'Lose yourself in / impulse buys, second-hand Faust, neon zines / and feeling, feeling you could die / here in this beautiful museum: / t'was now, t'was then.' The division between now and then is one of many that structure these works. Other divisions also offer spaces that can be not only acknowledged but luxuriated in. Deng travels in time and space into the lives of Brahms, backpackers and Monet, 'knee-deep, beyond what he could see'. She travels across generational misunderstanding in the poem 'a conversation', which expresses even in its layout on the page the divisions between expressiveness and propriety, solace and solitude, mother and daughter. There is a beauty and solace in the movement across the divide and in the understanding that fills in the silences, but there is a beauty, too, in the acknowledgement of difference and in the space that is held open on the page. These are measured poems, balancing presence and absence, past and present, detail and abstraction, relish and reflection, questions and answers. Like a Romantic poet, Deng is able to luxuriate in indecision, uncertainty, language heard as accent before understanding, heartbreak, volatility and insouciance. If for Lily Holloway, your twenties can flicker as two recurring seconds in time, for Modi Deng, your twenties are 'when you're given the confusing puzzle of / boundaries   that fall   in pleasant places   when waiting is as important / as having'.

These are three very distinctive poets, each of whom brings her own obsessions, knowledge and perceptions to the poetry collected in this volume. Yet there is a real resonance between the three selections. All three poets are interested in time, its rhythms and pacing and the distance it opens up between the present and the past. All three are interested in absences, spaces and erasure, and find their own ways of representing absence both in the words of the poem and in the ways they are laid out and expressed on the page. Solitude opens up possibilities for the exploration of self and for the recognition of others, for feelings to be felt and to pass on, for dreaming and for experiencing the beyond. The sublime can be 'aweful' but also enlightening, or endarkening, and the dizzy gravity of the world can be both exhilarating and comic. All three poets are keenly alert to the world's beauty, which can be found in hunching bridges, the radiance of stars, the stratification of time and place. I have loved travelling through the worlds evoked in these poems, some so familiar, some so remote, all so alluring.

Anna Jackson

Lily Holloway

a child in that alcove

Reverb or Aftermath

It happens
as a guest
latent or
underlying
like a needle
to the soft part
of your foot.
It happens
always
in hallways
my body
a monument
to never
forgetting.
It happens
all worlds
now
indented
even
the divots
of my spine.
It happens
and a child
runs backwards
rewinding
into
my chest.

bed against the wall

crawling past your ankles
at the bottom of the mattress
i am a fata morgana
an exercise in spreading thinly

i love you in the night-time
when the moon through the window
reflects on your lower lip
a lake, the lake

i think i can feel the reverberations of something further downstream

i am worried things will never be okay
because i slept all day
i woke wondering why i could hear the sea and thought maybe
the very tops of the trees were moving in the wind
just the very tops
but it was your laptop overheating

in the night i pull a fragile train behind me
a blanket trailing in earth
not like how illegally released koi
are dragged over the rocks
because they are ornamental and inedible
on their way to be put into the meat grinder on the back of a flatbed truck

i dream i am scooby doo from the original '69 version
in the supermarket of the afterlife where everything is free
and each drink is exactly what you need
but didn't know you needed
where you shoot rusted clockwork birds moving on rails around the castle walls
only to have them pop up again

a toaster is passed over my head and i tell my sister
to make her own ekphrastic postcards
and that koi skulls are sensitive to vibrations
they feel fingertips or bootlaces falling into the river
and flee in an orange rushing that you have to see to believe

commuting with angela

last night i walked   her dog   boots scuffing concrete solitude
glistening in puddles   pissing on laingholm poles

she is scared of slugs   those grey spotted tongues
        inching under porchlight
      towards her door   invasion   moving morning perspiration

hold her thigh   – not hard or that's charlie's horse
i'm driving   but slips hand into yours
        two fingers
        circle your pulse   to the backstreet boys

it is what it is
she says, *slugs pop like blisters* *rat lungworm burst forth*   *confetti larvae*

        and we cannot survive it

letter I will never post

I am still grieving the thing you took
so suddenly in that night

when the streetlamps
averted their
gaze

when my hands
got full of
fence

when my teeth
were clenched
apartments

where do I place this bouquet of small shames
so diligently gathered?

in your mother's laundry
basket?

in an essay on midsummer
night
dreaming?

do you carry a proud bag now
and may I ask what is in it?

a crumbling silk
or
tumbling skylines
or
a child in that
alcove?

periphery

there is a blur on the edge
of the rock pool on
the surface of a taut and
under-hanging globe
of green there are fish
suspended in their darting
under your shadow
children hiding in the
cupboards and archways
your mass has laid down

i didn't know who you were

i thought i had deleted
the photos of you but there you are

at the edge
of a picture of the sunrise
a knee in the corner a hand
on the breakfast table not even
just an empty silhouette – this
might have been okay – but a
flurry of wings a hiss
of bus at stoplight
the breaking of thick
pottery i have been here
for years and i know
it will never be home

you're standing over
standing over my river

in the same spot each time

around

as the tide

i am walking the path
around hobson bay point
nasturtiums grow up the cliff face
and the pitted mud has a scattering
of thick jagged pottery, bricks
faded edam cheese packaging
and a rusty dish rack
all of the green algae
is swept in one direction
i am aware of the blanketed crabs
only when a cloud passes overhead
and they escape in unison
into their corresponding homes
claws nestling under aprons
my dad talks about my depression
as if it were the tide
he says, 'well, you know,
the water is bound to go in and out'
and to 'hunker down'
he's trying to make sense of it
in a way he understands
so he can show me his working
i look out to that expanse,
bare now to the beaks of grey herons,
which i realise is me
in this metaphor

i am desired

i am twelve years old at a sleepover
i eat the whole tub of ice cream
and omegle's black rectangle types:
tell the girl in blue to take her dress off
my dress has a wide zipper
that tracks its way down my back
teeth cold against the divots of my spine
(i wear it to my first ever date
with a boy who tells me
i look better with my hair up)

facebook keeps advertising me t-shirts
with hyper-sexualised velma dinkleys
splayed on the ground, hands grasping
(i can't see without my glasses!)
or bent over and licking the magnifier
i always liked how she solved the mystery first
and held it under that big orange turtleneck
like the reveal was something she owned

my twenty-second year
flickers like the same two seconds
of a deep river, over and over
in those two seconds
i cannot take a full breath
and my body does not feel like a home
it doesn't feel like much of anything
except maybe a concrete ruin
just the frame of something that used to stand
in the middle of nowhere
witnessed only by the trees growing
and falling and rotting and growing again

don't disturb me, don't disturb me, i say
i am healing a deep slow burn

return again

1. two pigtails
2. one blue pantry door
3. port hill knees
4. postcards with dolphins
5. turn in your car seat
6. return again

1. hall no more
2. bumblebee grave
3. four acorns in my palm
4. five spittle bugs in that bush
5. quiet spaces when i return
6. return again

1. hand on corrugated fence
2. see estuary heron
3. seven crumbed mushrooms in a paper bag
4. thirty-six ice plants blooming on the dunes
5. a shrek boogie board over them
6. return again

1. discovery centre
2. there is no box of bees
3. there are still jars of pipi
4. one japanese butterfly collection
5. two basins for sand to go
6. return again

1. two plumes of breath
2. a scattering of rosehips
3. one school pool under blue tarpaulin
4. stand in the rain
5. feel the weight of yourself
6. return again

you are my night terror i hope i am yours

open my mouth and sand spills out in towers and slipping hills endless
open my mouth and vomit is shot at speed chunks of green monopoly
houses marbles clumps of drain hair and pineapple lumps open my
mouth and i scream magpies robbing mutton sobbing and gasping who
go for eyes pimples scabs making meaty nests open my mouth and i
turn inside out filling bathtubs with puddles of mouthwash and sperm
cilia grasping out motherless open my mouth and i'll bite your tongue
off with my judge judy teeth and swallow open my mouth and i bleed
uterus lining through my trousers and it's got teeth in it gunky pva
blood and pubes open my mouth and i'll give you a terminal illness
with slug intestines full of rat lungworm popping and you'll run
shrieking kettle open my mouth and i'll tell you of metallic streetlights
cervical scrapings scraped knees and ego death open my mouth and my
uvula is snakes and i'm on the temple floor spilling open mosaic open
my mouth and i'll feed you translucent opal larvae that do nothing but
stare open my mouth and out tumble severed ears and none of them
match hemorrhoids fibroids and cysts cascading like old-school candies
open my mouth and out spurts piss and scalding hot coffee open my
mouth and hear dido swinging by her neck in the throne room open
my mouth and your head is a cyst and i'm multitasking driving the
northern express committing hit and runs on the harbour bridge open
my mouth and grip hangnail with teeth ripping it up to the elbow open
my mouth and i'll whisper you ate the twin in the womb slapping you
into torn stockings under freight truck wheels open my mouth and
watch me floss until i slip and hit skull keep flossing my face a bone
carving open my mouth and i know your porn of choice a gif of taylor
swift tripping in heels open my mouth and your veins are throbbing
crimson clotting and you desperately screech in pak'nsave air only siren
moons blot in and out of eyesight and we're watching we're all fucking
watching blood thickening in you hissing shoppers staring blank-eyed
over stopped trolleys convulsions and bare concrete floor.

stocktaking during venlafaxine discontinuation

head: there is a layer of air pressing upwards between brain and skull
like if you apple cored my temples i would deflate a little
mind: holds canyons; i dream there are birds nesting in the hedging; a tally
going up really fast
eyes: dour cow eyes, the kind that look up through lashes; i see granules
dissolve in my coffee and am reminded that whitebait are many
species
ears: when i typed i'm so in lobe with you; hearing the one leaf in the
wind on the driveway; i dig a capsule hotel in the white noise
and fall asleep within it
mouth: a flatbed truck; a slap; there is a warning in the mass death of eels
teeth: not suitcases; bared like aegis
chest: the quietest panic attack happens when my heart is a small dog;
the bk coffee machine is cleaning itself and the screen that usually
plays music videos is just a list of files on a grey background
nipples: hard bits of gravel, the type that gets shunted in between
your boot gills and becomes part of the process
belly: full of proposals and kitchens
legs: rosehips, perhaps, descending; i am always blushing a path covered
in pebbles
feet: the female grays river grass moths don't fly; i remember
walking concrete through that expanse of car dealerships

a girl's name a headline

sackfuls of mothers tumbling   our baby hairs spread in
halos are arranged like dead people   laughs echoing out from cosy
                    sleeping bag breath

that thumping in her heart is a wrenching   a wrenching a wrenching
spinning compass-like   this starkness the exiting of a mall's movie theatre

jumping into abandoned trolleys
grinning wicked at the managers, holding hands
                                        jumping waves

water-logged clothes might   drown   us   playing horses in school
uniform pleats   catseyes cascade from pocket holes
          at home   eyelashes fall
                    and get lost in the carpet

pour out the libation thimbles   chop   off the least useful fingers
whisps behind locket doors   the tail of a kite and
     garlands of necks in the pantry
screaming in the four square car park I'm screaming   in
     the four square
               car   park and the automatic light
                                                  turns   on

it's dark then the lights   turn on and dad says
                              i have a tongue like a razor

Box kite

Driving over the Auckland Harbour Bridge
in my girlfriend's little white zipper
I thought I saw a box kite
in the drizzling rain over the yachts.
I'd only ever seen box kites in movies
with families on green hillsides
or in that book
Detective Peabody Up in the Air.
But looking back over my shoulder I realised
it wasn't a box kite
(those houses to small blocks of wind).
It was a large golden helium balloon
in the shape of an S
tumbling upwards towards the grey lid of clouds
revealing unseen currents by being buffeted around in them.
It probably goes without saying
that I wondered where it came from
what unfinished phrase it left behind

 ale or avings!

 eize the day or cyber ex!

 abotage or hi trionic

a uit
a co t
a di continuation
a cholar
a chip on my houlder

a uck
an abu e
a quare
a wim instructor
 ilence or a

a te t
a fal ehood
a fore t
 pringing into action
 weet 16!

Sentries

I’m frantically chasing my mother who weaves in and out of the aisles
throwing down craft supplies. I trip over scissors and quick unpicks

not seeing her face, only clean ponytail and collar poking out over plum
cardigan. We run between shelves of antique vases but lose contact with
the linoleum

and float out. In this world we drive couches like cars. I'm picking one up
from the junkyard with a blue shag cushion for reference. Bumper stickers
are glinting

while the couches lie gridlike. We scramble through the drivers’ seats
running fingers through the upholstery. In the winter gardens there are
fish tanks

nestled between succulents. One has a tangle of thin eels within it. Boys tap
on the home of a solitary neon tetra until it shatters. I hold the fragments
together

and try to keep the fish swimming in a handful of glass and water. They put
me in the newspaper. I run out to catch you in the ocean, my mother

but you keep dipping under. As I look around I notice, embedded in rock
formations are those white plastic fans, not rotating anymore just facing
the horizon.

Is any of this relevant?

A camera pans right revealing
overlapping tides superimposing
supermarket tiles and I see locals
swallowing giant kauri snail shells
thus completing historical courtships
either that or they wear them on their hips.

I suppose beginnings are laborious to construct.

Meanwhile,
somebody keeps carving chairs
out of trees while they're still living
I sit above in a banana tree surrounded by snakes
and can tell the maker is dissatisfied
leaving trails of unfinished seats behind them.

What is the link between event and after-effect?

I swim out to a basketball floating in the lake
(it's still got room 18 written in vivid)
and touch the hand of a dead body
reaching up from the weeds
I am a dog so it doesn't matter much
the camera zooms in on my wet fur.

Impossible to grasp the temporality of these moments.

There is always a hair on the backwards
left quadrant of my tongue
the shelf that tastes bitterness
it's either yours or the cat's
but tonight i am a coconut crab
in a suburban pool
claws just reaching above the surface.

There is no real certainty of origin.

I see you at 3 a.m.
in the Four Square carpark
howling with your animal mask on
I am stuck in the car and you are approaching
I know because the camera focuses
on the rearview mirror.

The timeline is elusive.

The only type of intimacy you can grasp
is mass-produced like named keychains
on stands that swivel
in all of the souvenir stores
and the audience can tell
you are the type who will be alone.

Nothing is devoid of meaning.

Up the hill in the old town
a red barn is attached to a library
large spiders are roaming over
the jungle gym and into mailboxes
on another channel
the basements of local craft stores
call a low hypnotic drone
telling you to chase butterflies.

There is no end to possible meanings.

The past colours the present
in a way that cannot be grasped
like a cheap child's wristwatch

(a colourful character travelling
around the centre point
pointing at the hours with oversized gloves)
like waking up not knowing
which life you are living today.

There are no page numbers.

She wonders aloud why the sky is so pink
but it's not, you say
maybe she's looking at a sky that has passed
a passenger to heritage or history
inaccessible to you.

My narrative is self-interrupting.

I reach out the side of the final frame
unhook the images from words
so meanings get out of sync
the whole thing
a relay of missed connections
truncated conversations
a tragedy, really.

hopscotch

cul-de-sac children draw winding hopscotch thinner and thinner up the hill
after the rain it's a faded tapeworm, segments curving in and out
i see it 'cause i am walking myself and it's that time of night
when the grass beetles dash across the pavement towards the other damp green
my brain is that hairy maclary book, the one with chaos at the vet
and i can't stop thinking about the parallels between smurfette and biblical eve
i unclip my skull like a sistema lunch-box and it's full of stick insects
who scuttle through a rip in the screen door as if it is double-time
out under the dripping bush and into those pumice holes
before the isolation, my girlfriend and i midnight-wandered
on takapuna beach and there was a duck in the rolling waves
she had two ducklings tumbling behind her illuminated by phone flashlight

a lulling / it's stratified, you know

bring me those lacy bed jackets
of '60s housewives
the ones with the ribbons unravelling
so the threads lie
between heavy
divisions of territory

it crawls out of my mouth like something that's settled
like you could imagine swinging an axe
into her trunk
like you could get lost in a copse
of her body
tripping over yourself

lift up a log and out comes scurrying

the thickness

a blanket of black legs
amplifying the canopy

layers excavated
of kererū, tree-rat
cicada shell and lichen

meanwhile
the bruise under my eyebrow has ripened
vessels unable to hold

the harvest
which is ample

juices breaking membranes
dripping from pinpricks with stick

-iness

bees fall slowly

drunk on just sip

-ping

moirai

i) clotho
pulled out of thumb endless i am
knuckleward and they call me a wheel
i am they call me a wheel you pull
across cheekbones to feel what type of plait
i am spinning tightness tightness and they drag me
dough between spread fingers i feel them call me a wheel
see the pith of the orange stretching between i'm
gelatine melting into strings
sleekness beneath my belly they call me a wheel thinning

they call me a wheel churning tarmac
rolling mossy slips and landslides

they call me a bobbin they call me spin cycle

they call me a wheel spinning in the parlour
teeth
bleeding
i
am
drawing
blood
from
stone
i
am
that
suck
of
the
needle
pulled
nurseward
buticannotandwillnoticannot and will not be umbilical cord i cannot and will

not bediscordant i am a single note calling i ama single note icy they call me a wheel but i must thread the needle and they call me a wheel but they call me pan dora and they call me a wheel with f ingernails on fire and they call me their origin a nd they call me their wheel and they call me predestine d and they loveme for winning and they love me for winning but they call me a wheel crushing fingers of children they call me a wheel

ii) lachesis
sat in front of fire   only weaving   only weaving   i am a
narrator   not listening at the door not
basement knitting i am   and   i   am
motherlines but mother's locked in the
about my day   they call me a tapestry taught down
dry   they call me a tapestry but they have not asked me

behind curtains and the moths have been   sucking   me
weaving snakes between columns   they call me a tapestry
dripping silkiness on the welcome mat   they call me a tapestry

they call me a tapestry   they call me a tapestry torn
they call me a tapestry   hanging in the hallway
friendship
bracelets
sewing
baskets
of
meat
fat
tectonic
etchings
i
stretch
and
bind
your

hands
tea
cosy
and im bindingandbindingandbindingandbinding and my knuckles are bleeding andbleedingandbleeding and im seepingseepingandseeping into the history cracks when men see me they imagine me weaving our bodies when men see me they imagine me doing their laundry when men see me they call me a tapestry when men see me they call me a tapestry when men see me they see me knittingthem backtogether and they call me a nightgown and they call me a tapestry and they call me a tapestry and they call me a tapestry and they call me fresh carpet and they see me inside them and they call me a tapestry and they call us inseparable and they tie me around their pinkies but i have learnt how to unpick my mother taught me to unpick but i have learnt how to defrost and i have learnt fingerknitting and they are watching my needles they are watching my needles but they call me their saviour and they call me a tapestry but i'm

iii) atropos
above   the   fire
all the trinkets are stuffed i am a sword on the wall
seas let's drown in depths we have not   seen
                                and   they call me a sword jumping

fly in windless nights leaf
hands so   loose   they   rip and rib
on the roof i say they call me a sword stretch
out   pull   me   out vibrating i want   out so get me   out i'm
pounding

pavement rhythms into skulls   they call me a sword get   me
they call me a sword   they call me a sword pounding

they call me a sword   sheathed in gut lining
above   the   fire
swerve

your
sweet
neck
can't
help
but
snip
those
thick
staples
let
drip
the
night's
oil
getitoutofmyheadicannotthink orsleep forbeingwrangledand i cannot be here icannotbehere but i am and ic annot leave for this is whereihave ended up everynight for weeks and theycallme a sword but i forget and i cannot rememberhow to graspthe h andle and i'm there in the pocket of night unable to unzip th ebeanbag from around my face and it's suffocating stars and they call me a sword but when i look in the mirror all i see is sheet metal and they call me a sword but they've never felt my ribs squeaking and they call me a sword but they are not bread makers and they call me a sword but don't know my emery they call me a sword but they call me a sword

the field

i am lying on a field
in the freshly minted spring sun
across the way there are tennis players
like ants on a wall

a body puts a rugby ball down
runs ten widths
i am in the part of the field
where the dew is now evaporated

i practise changing the focus of my eye
in: my cardigan fibres
out: the field
in out the space between
in out all of the webs

lacuna and periphery
where blades touch

all in the field

the daisy
the leaf
the hummus pot

all players

pegasus gateway motel
(before ali's funeral i make my mum cry)

through the motel's
net curtains of whimsy
one may position themselves
in relation to mum's silver
odyssey people-mover

i cannot see it for i am under the duvet
digging nails under my cheekbones
into those overripe peaches
until i feel the moment of deserved
puncture

my face drips and the bees
who lilt around the room
on their quavers, bumping gently
against the microwave door
are drunk on just sipping
from the crescents

my thirteen-year-old body
imagines dying of sheer will
imagines exploding like a dandelion
and disappearing on the wind
i hold my breath

when the motel is asleep
i walk over the dunes
sit in soft sandy divots
among the toroheke
body folded like a tea towel

i pick up a beached starfish
blue skin callous under thumb
its cilia no longer grasping out

throw it back home to the tide
i pick myself up again

in the morning over continental cornflakes
all is forgiven
mum examines my face closer
the sand not yet warm
from the chill

methods of burial

fantastic or grotesque pottery with elaborate handles
never depict the movement of cattle
up the hill in summer and down the hill in winter
only inhumation [being final disposition] and cremation

fosse [being trench]
and pozzo
like shafts in the turf
bodies vertical

we are drinking and drinking and screaming on the palatine hill
the air awash with typefaces
i am garamond and you are something else serif
and our feet crush through the urns

using a can opener we detomb my grandmother
but she's just a breastplate and dappled sky
experts try to identify what type of breastplate she is
and, in doing so, when people first settled on the plateau by the river

we consider resomation [being dissolved in a bullet]
and an ossuary [a second destination] but i already have thighs
like a memorial reef
concrete and remains in tango, fish swimming in and out of my archways
sea anemones resting in my dimples

we decide on being woven into a mushroom suit
being eaten by the pervasive network
mycelium fingering like bone sponge
laying down toes and spreading them

the road to the hill is closed

i was a warning
in the mass death of eels
i was a poem
not yet a poem
but a tangle
i ran
down the margin
of their sleek bodies

i was collapse
where they huddle under
arches
i was historian i was
narrative trajectory
an arrow dipped
in crimson
i was slipping

over fields
when the rain
slicks grass down
i was that thick
muscular writhing
mirroring fence lines
along the anatoki
to the swimming hole

i was the boulder
grinding along the bed
i was the flood
into the morning
i was the grid
of an ancient city
snapped along
perforated edge

i was a child
in the main house
not yet that child
but the staring
into bonfires
out of windows
over the kitchen
sink

departures

taken from G.G. Ramsay's translation of Juvenal's Satire III

retreat

to perpetual
falling

let out

Muses
a-begging.

little

Daedalus

slipping a

Farewell

horn-blowers

and

entrails

carry

no

accomplice—

the sands

and the

trulls

in

slippers

worm

a torrential

rope-
dance

recline upon

the
flattery
of

ecstasies

the

maiden

unpolluted

and feared

ladies

of
the wall

may

keep

dishes

of

coarse

woes

Here

a

breast
pallid

and worshipful

lip

full of

men

tumble

nothing to

bed

Tru Paraha

in my darkling universe

we shred 12 unconsciousnesses

echo)))locate DNA marooned

invisible maw accretes dark god   perpetually astral

how quasar   how quick this ejaculat

'm utterly spaghettified

i liquid feed a beast

forgetness& warped singularity

Te Taiwhetukii   he huna

imbibe helium much [= bwaha]

chirrrp   ,,,,,,,,,,,,,,,,,,,,,,,,,,,,,,,,,,,,,,

perturbed how he died quite lively

primordial spooling what the actual

strands of atoms ki tua

o te once upon their bodies collide

graze ellipsoidal galaxy

baryonic matter juts a creamy backbrain

      sigh

no light survives ‘the end of time’

swill   carnivals of particles

mephitic pseudo-fragrance making

                                        dizzy grav~~it~~y

submerge porohita uriuri exceeding stars

a billion times multiply more than one trillion

               eon upon aweful eon

Abell 85

J2157

Sagittarius A*

Pōwehi   hell (o) earthlings

CYGNUS X-1

HR 6819

he memed a dream constituent quite otherly

she thinned into fizz

ghoul suns roaming galactic

astronomic uncertainty collapsed

love you linger space all xeroed

aerosphere like corpse gism

extruding limbless anemones what a

superradiant massive !

binary-tethered blackest blackness on black

we suckle Kurawaka clit

ore us fathomless let’s get woo woo

radio waves ,,,,,,,,,,,,,,,,,,,,,,,,,,covert roaming nuclei

,,,,

this ever tipsy Ioverse

luminosity rotisserie   turns quantum fuzz

you know its spin its soft emissions

      infinitely compressed bright meat

we slow-moed we sped

      lasso-wrangled bouncy castles rogue

fully ascendant & frame-dragging

ultraviolet violence *like there's no tomorrow*

-... . -.-- --- -. -.. | -.-. ..- .-.. - ..- .-. .

ki tua

-... . -.-- --- -. -.. | ... .-.. . . .--.

ki tua

-... . -.-- --- -. -.. | -... .-.. --- --- -..

ki tua

-... . -.-- --- -. -.. | -.-. .. ...- .. .-.. | -.. ..- .. - . ...

ki tua

-... . -.-- --- -. -.. | -.. --- --. -- .-

ki tua

-... . -.-- --- -. -.. | . -. - . .-. .--. .-. .. ... .

belong

-... . -.-- --- -. -.. | .-.. . --. . -. -..

beyond

-... . -.-- --- -. -.. | - . .-. .-. --- .-.

beyond

-... . -.-- --- -. -.. | .... --- .- -..-

beyond

-... . -.-- --- -. -.. | . -.-. --- -...- .--. .-. --- -.. ..- -.-. .

beyond

-... . -.-- --- -. -.. | -.. --- ..- -... -

-... . -.-- --- -. -.. | -... --- -.. .. . ...

be gone

-... . -.-- --- -. -.. | .... --- .--. .

beyond

-... . -.-- --- -. -.. | --.- ..- .- -. - ..- -- | .--. .... -.-- ... .. -.-. ...

beyond

-... . -.-- --- -. -.. | .- -- -... .. ...- .- .-.. . -. -.-. .

-... . -.-- --- -. -.. | - .- .-.. -.- .. -. --.

-... . -.-- --- -. -.. | .--. --- ...- . .-. - -.--

-... . -.-- --- -. -.. | --. . -. -.. . .-.

-... . -.-- --- -. -.. | - .- .-.. . -. -

-... . -.-- --- -. -.. | .. -. ...- .- ... .. --- -.

-... . -.-- --- -. -.. | .-.. --- ...- . | ... --- -. --. ...

-... . -.-- --- -. -.. | .--. --- .-.. .-.. ..- - .. --- -.

-... . -.-- --- -. -.. | .-- .- .. - .- -. --. ..

-... . -.-- --- -. -.. | .- .--. .--. .-.. .- ..- ... .

-... . -.-- --- -. -.. | ..-. ..- -. -.. .-. .- .. ..-. ...

-... . -.-- --- -. -.. | .--. --- . - .-. -.--

-... . -.-- --- -. -.. | .-. . ..-. ..- --. .

-... . -.-- --- -. -.. | .--. --- .-. -. --- --. .-. .- .--. .... -.--

-... . -.-- --- -. -.. | .-.. .- .--

-... . -.-- --- -. -..

zerow

ki hea

;;;

thigh bone pavilion

en

tangle tan angel

staccato g-s pots

dreamtime broth   . . .

e ipo (i te pō ask sky

alien awaken her)e   ?

torn light

slayed rapture   0

everwhere

death s cent

Waiotara

Puhata

Ngunguru

Tautari

Taurua

Hau

Pari

Erana

teera taawera ka marewa i te pae ______________________________

1. Ngaati Kahu Kupenga

greatgreatgreatgreatgreatgreatgreat

greatgreatgreatgreatgreatgreat

greatgreatgreatgreatgreat

greatgreatgreatgreat

greatgreatgreat

greatgreat

great

grand

you are witnessing an execution, stunning in its detail

the golds could've been scraped off Cleopatra's vulva or a
flame-haired Klimt

you have to pick up groceries, pound fern root, swap
kids - a shame you can't stay

when the axe falls, we will all sing cheers, count 3 days
1 star & open our eyelids again

the naked one bleeding out robes - a casual acquaintance
of yours - says he knows what you did last summer
   give him a call

you have become pristine, your house immaculate as teeth

we're waiting to see if roses bloom from the scarlet ribbon
trail of his veins

i am craving watermelons just as you motion to stand
sluiced into torpid mouth pods

   angel
half of you is albatross & apples on the inside, your
scorched wing lashes my cheek as you pass as you pass

are you leaving? he has lost his head

pterodactyls circled the ten   there was Kawiti in

ferocious repose   cold wolfed their haunches

malingering   SW   curious beauty notched

about the dark places   dilated antennae

scanned a wall embossed with uncles ko wehe ki te poo

wingtipped fossils   where could his elegant death scene be?   stuffed boar

tohoraa   baby orangutan 17 years refrigerated cutest paws-tucked-up

pose Tyrannosaurus Rex's tuaraa tricked out with wires and

their real bones flailed the earth

tamariki danced smeared in merriment of charcoal
hours glared the sun we tunnelled fed with flowers
oils silicon hearts discovered by a moa trees with
superior memory archive us petrified into the ages

time & there was no time

every brand
of love no sign of the beloved

orchards full of aaporo
a thousand muzzled mouths

we being the core-bitten
legacy of every fallen one

v

t

t a v a

a

[redacted] would not normally participate under the circumstances participant y prefers to be called Mihiatukiatanenuiarangituturuwhakamauakiatina or [redacted] for short participant y recommends a meat-only diet participant y is fond of neighborhood cats participant y looks best after a near-death experience participant y wishes to remain anonymous for the purposes of this [redacted] participant y complains of insomnia participant y assumes a champagne lifestyle on a beer budget participant y has friends in low places participant y dreams of [redacted] participant y is leaving the premises participant y will toss you at the drop of a hat participant y spent a brief time incarcerated just casually participant y could do with a [redacted] participant y has never met a great g r e a t g r e a t grandparent participant y could be here today gone tomorrow participant y insists on privacy at all times when out in public participant y does not recognise your government participant y talks quietly amongst themselves participant y dances like a 3-legged donkey participant y stings like a bee participant y is known for all kinds of carry-on participant y finds it more joyful to receive than to give participant y could be lovingly described as [redacted] participant y can barely hold down a job participant y has the makings of a great participant participant y has no racial preference in [redacted] participant y cannot abide talkback radio participant y has rolled people in their own homes participant y possesses a studious nature and inquisitive mind participant y appreciates your [redacted] participant y keeps in touch with family for birthday money participant y receives treatment from a physiotherapist participant y exudes a powerful performance presence participant y was brought to you by an unknown third party participant participant y invented Polga – a new craze in pole dancing and yoga participant y politely declines your kind offer participant y refuses to be [redacted] during this inquiry participant y is chatty loves horse rides and French cuisine participant y has a decidedly masculine build participant y relies on its [redacted] wherever possible participant y appears unsure of the terms of this agreement participant y demonstrated similar concerns in the past participant y regularly consumes [redacted] participant y observes a modest dress code participant y tried [redacted] once only once participant y has a wonderful rapport with children participant y dabbles in languages participant y supports [redacted] participant y has been hailed participant y occasionally defecates on Herne Bay properties participant y strongly believes that [redacted] matters participant y is a high achieving Work and Income fail story participant y longs to one day own an armchair participant y studied at a reputable [redacted] school participant y has never been to Dunedin participant y could easily be a hand model participant y swears to tell the truth the whole truth and nothing but the [redacted] participant y looks down at you as we speak participant y sees dead people participant y sends its regards participant y was delivered through a C-section participant y is a few kuumara short of a haangi participant y knows someone who used artificial assisted reproduction technology participant y is of indeterminate age participant y invites you to fully participate participant y has an atheist slash post-humanist slash Judeo-Christian thing going on participant y says "[redacted]" a lot participant y has a questionable accent participant y prefers to have no pants on participant y enjoys cryptic crosswords participant y struggles with [redacted] thresholds participant y has a tidy bedroom participant y is an award winner of critical acclaim participant y created an unsuccessful website participant y is widely read and well travelled participant y enjoys a good pie participant y would choose the sickness benefit over a nine-to-fiver any day participant y has tested [redacted] therapy participant y would have you believe there is no such thing as participant y participant y wishes you all the best participant y never imagined being here right now not ever participant y may choose at any time to discontinue participation within this [redacted] participant y stays home and saves [redacted] I am not participant y [redacted] girl

nonchalant

blue-dark

girl

reach

steel

girl

arms

vast

pressing.

huge

trees

her

swo**o**ped

bra**n**ch

owl-lik**e**

grave

lover

darkly

moonrise

velvet

hooted.
scraped
        stars

one-ribbed

girl
        swaying
        dark-edged
                storms.

green

tulip

head

and

lay

aga**i**nst

sandalled

whi**t**e

gr**a**ss.

st**i**r

he**r**.

words

green

wind

universe rant
immacculate womb
        i die infinitely
star particle reborn

beyond chorus of extinction distinctly resounding by forest **lake** swamp
        skin offering
beside furrowed bean pea beet **potato** courgette near Bastion pā bunkers
        to church palisade
behind middens broken glass backyard state digs inside temple pothole
        terrestrial **cave**
atop mountain hiccupping vegetal thunder across continent romance tectonic
        hot plasma
over **trail** of ancestor revolutionary quest within border line territory
        hundred rank priestesses
beneath province town village neighbourhood armour under **sky** bird leaf
        weaving
between pounamu doors of peace flag descendant around **flower** field shimmers
        colour scent hue
around blue planet **atom** incorrigible tomb between quantum existence
        tomorrow's return
under current flow reign rip unorthodox **tide** beneath parameter endogenously
        made-in-NZ
within seagull bowels aftermath to a feasting over terraces **bat** cravings
        latent artillery
across silage sea **shark** wild ray piranha inside crater red **scoria** where
        cattle graze
behind skull valley croonings elusive insomnia near sub-urban landscrape
        excavation trash
beside viaduct **carbons** ceremonial breathtank by **adzes** discovering new
        island

to a sleepwalker freedom oceanic wet dreaming

in the belly of the paradox

in the nerve-spine of the conundrum

at the lip of the precipice

at the turn of the golden century continuum

to one divine origin progressively revealing by **sperm** whale beached on indelible **sand**
beside musket-death warrior nursing moist **seed** near convoluted politics urban drift thesis
behind unveiled **dawn** maiden deadly inheritor inside dancing trenches such **peach** ripe wonder
atop sky tower tongue piercing steel leviathan across **kauri** blood gum dug **sweat** wilderness
over land women lost art buried **semen** within tenuous griefs our flung far carrions
beneath placenta **tree** nourishes future prophecy under lore of continuance hope omnipotent
between lovers agape in deep **flesh** mystery round eye-petalled children blinking dark unity

in the belly of the paradox

in the nerve-spine of the conundrum

at the lip of the precipice

at the turn of the golden century continuum

watched
once

the sun
the moon

make
love

fuck o

bled
celestial

orgasm
into

clouds

and then

blue genocis   Taawera inception
        preserve its deathless ,coo ,coo
she's labile in animal outers   polyamide
        iPhone scales his lifeline uh-
                                oh smashes and cracks

crows wrangle a tree   or frack these
        clouds im possibly stopped
                        toxic exotica ,metrospectral
        love of skyglow wow
t heir spring greens dismembered nightly
        Raakaunui   light   trespasses
                                        awoke & watered

                Te Poo-maa   whitening   slinks out an outfit
                        teeraa Puanga kei runga raa
                how glaring perpetual haere mai   haere
                                        worship this miasma ,e koo ,e koo
                        kua whetuurangitia

1. as i turn you turn me onto

2. a cold, slow violence wrings the moon's neck

3. everything in threes

a halo beyond the haze & how it shined .unidentifiable birds alerted though discreet my way of moving (cue Tangotango & the stars) .chill and suppurate speeches ,but wouldn’t retreat till i embrained this light its pathological sprawling .took a snap that turned out bad you would have nursed with vivid filter ,noise reduction ,being kind .Stellarium sees what i cannot believe what i can’t

.time over ,you ,among the brights .a menacing pained my scapulae till immobilised i .gazed gazed and exclaimed all clever flesh - soon passed out .the grief ,then greyscales roiling above and across and was left .Sky & co. incorporated looked fake asf you’d never say it to their surfaces :they grant us an honorary emoji of astrology for detecting sexo-celestial correlates during isolation ;herein directs your erectness

.according to my lunar phase hominids prevail .binocs arrive by courier amid Oorongonui ,Mauri and Mars we deep augment for hours ,hours pass .later ,she tuned its blues to ambers ,endangered antihistamine .ae concur ,let’s penetrate all night then set my clock to NZST for soft apocalypse .heliacal ,we rise & rise (their eyes expire)

pages freeze
in cryosphere
fitted sheet ov darknyss
          odouring
tw itter rank cadaverous

scapula might
          kiss
a bit eclipxical riff

where ache too ocular
fecund air
          poeit say
ghost-flesh a cloud

accentuate ur
          miniature killer
nightscape un-coded
lOverse
how assassin blanket

love@ or
such body rapt
here bl ck n ng

unleft w*
xhume wh longing outrig
distances

was where this had they
mind in (dyslx

suicidal deepspace
metasex mourn out
            dark script
come   ._
            lie with

greyscale flaunt
navel raid   thaws
            would it ever be
so, if

stalactite brood on site
            collar d
rainbow-dripped grief pits
'refrigerated weepery'
etc.

            molecule
prettiless meat sacks
suck epiphany
            when black
complicit & light was &
body opaque

reek star by th caveload

skull our
noir mineral ether-
net sharded
ephemera what kind i's

delirious #corpsing
skin gratuity insert
an atom y
frequent elderspeak

procurate
backbrain foetal glitter
wwhhhh* ** *****

i 2 am left-hand
scribe
thought-rot revelling
cryptic what h* decay

contusion
to th

ripped slumber
into therex swallowd
horizon-till now
gl acial
*
* *
*
* w *
* i

* *
* * * a

* * *
x
*z

k
* * m
y *
*
* *
* * h
* *
* * *
* * q
* e
b
c
j
*
*

* *
* r

k *

3 a.m. cosmos
ash sense seer
amphibiat evernyss
silenc
e

whatof gurgl ng
desire-tree$ midnight sword
to plasma

l*fe
abyssl horrorific

mist whisperd `~
whir real delirium `~
s[oh]s

wheniwasacannibal lifewasalotmorepositive,peopleamicable. icoulddemolishanentirecarcassinonesittinglickingthegra viedventricleattheendofeachmeal.discussionswerealotless political.nobodyostracisedmefromtheirhomeorforgotmyinvi tetotheendofyeardinner.icouldstillattendchurchinmysunda ybestanddrinkofthebloodandeatofthefleshlikearegularsinn er.friendsdidn'thidetheirkidsorsleazyrelatives.iwasn'tt hefamilyfreakjustbecauseienjoyedadifferentcutofmeat;iwa swaitedonhandandfootsotospeak.thenibecameavegetarianand ofcourse*noone*wantedtoknowme.you'dthinkihadkilledsomeone

in a d rk energy dominated
universe space itself
xpands and xpands and
th centre of infinit i is
anywhere th body
will

or so it was

stellar corpse burn blue annihil
unearthly yr optics pulsate

reach toward all thought of it ko t pae tawhiti

whāia kia tata a a a a

bury my heart on Mars design hr cataxcomb whatif
they scatter fine ashes amongst th veil

i hereby explode & will th remains to remain

archive these prettiful hues i don t rotate each day to become forensic waste

sh sighs
glitters is gold

further away they are th further away we are from them
& stuff or close enough
*rolls eyes 90° clockwise in orbits

in hs impossible dream   passing th speed of light ka mihi atu ki ngā whetūrere

saw wilding frights
invisible from its outsides a dimple in th fabric memory
of its mass   ‘te ana o Whiro’ warping one-way door

too coruscated you longed to die historically &
did

fell into a bock hell   ball
choke

bleak loch

hello back

↘↘↘↘↘↘↘↘↘↘↘↘↘↘↘↘↘↘↘↘↘↘

↘↘↘↘↘↘↘↘↘↘↘↘↘↘↘↘↘↘↘↘↘↘

↘↘↘↘↘↘↘↘↘↘↘↘↘↘↘↘↘↘↘↘↘↘

↘↘↘↘↘↘↘↘↘↘↘↘↘↘↘↘↘↘↘↘↘↘

me he matakōkiri koe i runga / topa iho mai ki raro

on through to th other side

The Lazy Astronaut

atom of sloppy
to foamy plops
(my poop floats

)

Modi Deng

安慰 (an wei)

lessons

on freefall:

1 your eyes will water, and
2. you may emit silent *ooo* groans, like caterpillar smoke rings

on plants:

1. sometimes it's pertinent to look at the behaviour as well as
   understand its root
2. if you give me the space to grow, I will return to you my blossoming

on the cold:

1. two people and expectations that could
2. cut a roof in half

on breathing:

1. breath is to a phrase as a pulse is to rhythm
2. to come to terms with your feelings as you perform is to
   tumble headfirst, fists full of awkward vibes from the audience

on insouciant thoughts:

1. I don't mean to discredit hypnotherapy but I do
2. being passive means being a cavity for someone to fill

on words:

1. words are a celebration of the living and a balm for the dead
2. that's why the air softly eats up words when we
   break our hearts in-between

on Felicity:

1. I never expected to find a kindred spirit in '90s Keri Russell
   at first it was her volatile decision-making
2. but then it was her husky book sweaters
   her slinky slips and the steely grace of sometimes silence

on stories:

1. I want to be like my friend who smiles any time someone talks, hands resting under her chin
2. as if who they are is yet to unfold
   as if in that moment she sees how their childhood is still carrying them, limp and all

unrest

The prognosis for unrest
is poor, says the pendulum traveller
(he’s swung here before).
Longer than months stretching
to noon, longer than putting words
to a tune.

安慰 (an wei)

When light pooled in
the camber of your palm
and your quiet laugh dipped a reprieve, a catching net,
fullness to cheek hollow –
I couldn’t help it. Your candour was
embodied / your words fading /
our rhythm softly a morning moon.

Ben Lomond

Three people in the snow
two linked by marriage
            memorising fault line
                                    by fault line

and every now and again the head of the summit
tails in
    and out of sight

three people with backpacks and knees in the snow
threading the mountains with a silence
that once broken
            would make you cry

and every now and again the head of the summit
tails in
    and out of sight

like the early love of a June morning
first an accent and then the hearing
and the sky is a blanket wishing it gone

late on the summit a sparrow
whittling alone
                    and away

a conversation

my mother is not the type	to witness crying
and soften	to rush over
fluffy with concern	because she knows
each state is only a	liquid
dip into another	she sits there waiting for it
to be over	like how she bit her lips until
they bled during childbirth	because the nurse
told her to be quiet	how years of family
reinforced the division of	expressiveness
from propriety	daughter from
son	solitude
from solace	holding a book from
trying to hold up	the world.
I never understood this	divide always
saw her coolness as	distance never
grasped how	childhood grafts
lines deeper than	a well of years can wash
away until	last week when I
felt myself feel nothing	in order for something to pass
an attempt at survival	without the edges

what lies between the subject and myself

the first to leave was Camille and then his sight
but his shaky hands were sure on the easel and

by the banks of war
he kept at it
lopped off the darkness
and filled it with the milky edge of a cataract

the first to rise was the cool tulip-light of morning
the last to fall – dusk,
chrysanthemum seeds, loose soil –

broken Japanese counterpoint
the arched colonial bridge

in the middle he patched together plots like a
farmer's headache, polished the soot off the lily pads and
reared his own beauty. soon
he painted purplish bruises
white boater / white tux / whitebeard / maltese
muddied by imperfect sight

the bridges began to hunch over the winter gardens
his feet cracked while treading the tall path
and even though caution was advised
even though those who cup water are chosen for the army

Monet dreamed. he diverted the Epte and
dreamed knee-deep, beyond what he could see

priming his canvas with light and
mourning *after* life was a possibility

two artists who used to love
    one artist who still could
    lying on the grass but

afloat

tell me

Tell me
that funny story again. The one where I laugh in spades
and your voice wobbles as you speak
but you keep your cool. Better that than
the emptiness of falling through
memory, a thief through a skylight
stealthily, clumsily –
your voice keeps me here
as I listen, ae-o, ae-o, aeolian harp.

I was away, once, with salt tequila lemon
tying my tongue to sparkling water.
Distance comes with pretending you can cook
and the early mornings of slow, open fields. Quick, spin
your skirt around so the lady won't
see you desecrating Beethoven's
piano with your fingertips.
Eyes, your hand, sun, in mine. Lose yourself in
impulse buys, second-hand Faust, neon zines
and feeling, feeling you could die
here in this beautiful museum:
t'was now, t'was then.

My favourite moment in the Bible
is when Moses asks to see God's face.
It must be a basic human need, to search
and search unwarranted. I want so much to fill out sound
with my limbs and being,
my voice disappearing up the top
like a Slavic song.

now and then things come in tandem

write me into the dunes of your voice. lift me up and use kind words, like spirit, or radiant, or prayer. or hold me instead of speaking – this is our true stay. a little rain suffuses the garden and you ask if I live in the country and I say, no. it's just new zealand. we just have a valley that fills our window. you rest there, full of your strong-edged thoughts, and I think you are the nicest valley to rest in. I catch glimpses of us, mall window after mall window. mirror in your room. shy and tentative before we know the bridge of a nose or the soft flesh of a knee. before I memorise your worried pauses or the high-pitched space before you laugh. the air hums with it. before you carry me up onto your straw feet, trace a map with your hands. before you find huia bay and fold me in your hoodie. when it's too much I run and I run along the waterfront, fear and disbelief kicking into one. with hindsight perhaps I was cottony and too slow. you taught me to ask for recompense and to insist on my name. I picked up my contact lens shells and kept myself small and clean. but used your pillow and took too much. and at the end I left printed slippers the size of myself, curved and quiet and absent.

reflets

1. when they finally met her dad
a few months later
she dug her face into her mum's bony
blade of a shoulder. he looked different
with his long hair and he was so skinny, her
mum said. she went from swinging
an umbrella against the sun to swinging
on her belly at kindy. they made glitter
angels there, and she cried.

2. even in Timaru her mate Kate would
keep her photo beside her
bed. her mother supplemented her
with Centrum and current
events clippings and Mensa books. not once did
her maths teacher call her up on the fabricated
long division problems she couldn't see
she wondered about that. he marked each
of her problems, individually
and every day as she entered
her private school she slipped her glasses
deep down into her blazer pocket.

3. this refusal incurred the wrath of her mother
who had done the
same, albeit in university.
maybe she should have been like *I, Tonya* and
grown hard from it and tough. but she was soft
and eager to please, texting boys
test answers. at the optometrist
the blurry symbols held a
stamp of disapproval
problem child, she thinks. *my myopic eyes*
my crooked teeth.

4. she was promised that when she reached eighteen
she'd unfurl herself into
a butterfly
instead she hardened like sugar
molasses before the tongue
and simply carried on with the calves
of her dad and the
nerves of her
mum and as apples and oranges with
her brother

5. she imagines that music is a kernel
of strength. maybe she could grow roots
down into the earth
musty with garden moss and tarred
by the rain. shoot up sound and
space through her limited frame. touch a dimming
sky through a clothesline
blithe and happy with dirty feet and half-moon
lids. it wouldn't be tiring to go after
that, not at all.

6. there's not much to remember
from those earlier days. if you press her
hard enough maybe she'll
feel in her palms all the things her
hands have held –
glitter, tears, the softness of a daughter
like daybreak or a damp foal.
she'd see all that is
close to her and hold in hope all
that moves far away

today

today I am running without reason
without grief, or anger
sleeveless, without billowy
unwanted voices
today I am running because it is sunny outside
and the dog was so sweet
asking for one and
the sun flickers and enfolds the creek

there's / incoming / globby grey on the right
a shoulder lobe of sky and here I am
swerving underneath, phone a
dendrite of light
cutting up the same slope of film
I always do.

today I am just running
          asymmetrically
no understanding of how to separate relief
from deflation
still running my circuit of thoughts
so well-worn

I run here because it is in season
and the dog is walking
me. the speck of
my phone lost within the sunlight
that compounds
many many thousands of times. for a moment it
lacerates me and freckles
my face – pert, bright
but then I
push

through

tomorrow will be the same but not as this is

to a Colin McCahon painting, held in Te Puna o Waiwhetū

tomorrow I will dream
spend hours on one gleam of sky and its sound

melt away the Otago night, the
biscuity dark of its foreground

lay myself on a slate body of water
cold and curved, hollow and tailbone

all and while and remembering.

but before then I will
mix myself like so

smaller than a
leaf spine / smaller than space between

floorboards / smaller than sand
in black dripping

down into the linen of every day. and wait for a beam
to send me, onwards

lightning courses

give me some
more of your soft eyes
they crease
so well at the corners
they jump kerbs of thought
and soften your curly nape
of hair. they
compliment your
gangly elbows

they're a perfect match for my
soft (read: weak) heart
golly . . . apologising to bedposts I accidentally
kick and professing
to boys I purposely like and reading the
love parts of Russian novels

give me some more of your soft eyes
they make me paralysed, like
an exclamation mark (!)
they freeze-ray me when I come
down the stairs
and lull me into your Bach

you tip back your white
wine and every sinew
holds *energy energy energy*
and like furtive breaths
like lego steps your
soft eyes

field notes on Lewis Hyde's *The Gift*

in a few days I will be in Beijing
I will play in a hall and open outwards
like a gift
like the dizzying task of
one small tree trying to give the sun return
for what has entered it through a leaf (25)
this music will seep through every
moneyed crack and every rule
of every institution and
I will articulate what I have to say
unzip a slight gap between my chest of feeling
and my water-armed self, and in singing,
be free
in both (63)

Euston Road

suck a sample out,
like breath or a ragged memory
the needle pushes into the groove
and my skin puckers like gladwrap

everything is gone now –
everything my mother said to me

this is a vacuum incision –
the lady beside me has blue hair and a Northern accent
aggressively positive
then faltering and side-eyed.
she states that state healthcare
is free and whooshes with frustration when
they go beyond ultrasound
to biopsy.

it's confusing –
I lie there mask over jaw
thirteen hours behind
everyone back at home up
and waiting for me

everything is gone now –
my person, my fear

I'm only three months
due for an appointment. I walk
to Marylebone afterwards
mouth wrapping around the well-to-do word
balancing books unevenly
with a bag of heavy oily
noodles that lodge in the throat

leaving behind the paranoid clinical

attendants, all the pear-nurses and
the requisite burnt soya coffee
and I imagine my nerves smoking like
tendrils
repairing themselves

night

put my hand on your chest, a
gypsy-hungarian dance, offbeats
flexing your toes. teach me to
say things Matter of Fact,
how to open up, let go. show me how to wrap
rice in perilla leaves
wave the empty way giselle's
lover passes through her ghost arms, till at last their
fingers
catch, their legs an arabesque
crescent around each other. finding themselves
if only as night breathes its while.

in the intermittent break of day

in the intermittent break of
day is the soft down of
long arms and the way your nose always
surprised me because it isn't
wonky or pliable like mine

in the break of day is a montage of me
looking away to hide my feeling, and the same
zigzag along the webbing
of your knuckles like new skin
strange and cool and unfamiliar
maybe we should also try to cement your posture – bright and
strong, I thought, patient and understanding –

when I wake I'm left with your wrists
raised in theatrical gesture
your eyes that darken with the night, with
dreams like an arrow where you drive away and don't look
back and your hair that remains how it is
for years
except when morning comes

Brahms and his entourage

three years for a concerto
three years to write the longest
letter of his life. longer and clearer than all
his other paeans and
for the one who took the course of his feeling
and left it resigned
in its plight

he anchored the cello (his
plumb line) and measured chords in
ancient grey
he cupped his requiem in
floating, elated emptiness

and in the violet salon light
his invisible
entourage of sound streamed behind him
he left the room when it was
played to him

how it must be
to be caught by yourself

the eternal vespers

to the left of the piano is morning   freshly cut
like grass   here move unintuitive tendons   fingers
without muscle   here is stillness   the kind that fits into your own self
without unspooling another human's   evidently you are alone and evidently
you can think   sending thoughts upwards without reservations   like the
normalcy of a neck aching after you train   it's the radiant tug
of another day   grainy grip   ashen harmony   the silt noise
of a Dickensian street   and the weak but humming bird-
heart of everyone's twenties   when you're given the confusing puzzle of
boundaries   that fall   in pleasant places   when waiting is as important
as having   and time is just as revealing   as the heart
in the morning my English teacher walks past   as the tūī flings
out her line   and at night my brother sits opposite in a
rose plush chair   conducting me   grounding me
in strength of conviction   if it's a gift
then it's a gift   and to grow is to leave doubt behind   like the eternal
Scarlett on her Tara   raising up the next day

Notes

a child in that alcove

'bed against the wall' first appeared in *Poetry New Zealand Yearbook 2021*, Massey University Press, 2021.

'i think i can feel the reverberations / of something further downstream' first appeared in *Milly Magazine* and will appear in *Out Here: An Anthology of Takatāpui and LGBTQIA+ Writers from Aotearoa*, Auckland University Press, 2021.

'commuting with angela' first appeared as a part of the Given Words Competition for National Poetry Day 2019, where it was also translated into Spanish.

'letter I will never post' first appeared on the Caselberg Trust website as part of their international poetry competition.

'as the tide' first appeared in *takahē*.

'stocktaking during venlafaxine discontinuation' first appeared in *Scum*.

'a girl's name a headline' first appeared in *Midway Journal*.

'Sentries' first appeared in *The Spinoff* as part of 'The Friday Poem' series.

'moirai' first appeared in *The Three Lamps* and was later recorded for Paula Green's *Poetry Shelf*.

'pegasus gateway motel / (before ali's funeral i make my mum cry)' and 'methods of burial' first appeared in *Starling*.

'the road to the hill is closed' first appeared in *Poetry New Zealand Yearbook 2021*, Massey University Press, 2021.

in my darkling universe

A version of 'Postcard from Israel' was first published in *Poetry New Zealand Yearbook 1, 2014*, Massey University, 2014.

Versions of 'borderline', 'A. sky' and 'untitled #1' were first published in *Blackmail Press*.

A version of 'a Moanan theory of reality television' was first published in *Blackmail Press* and later appeared in *Best New Zealand Poems 2017*.

A version of 'paradox' was published in *Blackmail Press* and later appeared in *Puna Wai Kōrero: An Anthology of Māori Poetry in English*, Auckland University Press, 2014.

A version of 'Xero' was first published in *Tātai Whetū: Seven Māori Women Poets in Translation*, Seraph Press, 2018. It was translated into te reo Māori by Vaughan Rapatahana.

in my darkling universe takes its title with kind permission from the poem 'Your Being' by David Kārena-Holmes.

Recent works were conceived during a Michael King Writers' Centre residency in the summer of 2020.

安慰 *(an wei)*

'lessons' first appeared in *Starling* as 'Lessons II'.

'unrest' and '安慰 (an wei)' first appeared in *Starling*.

'Ben Lomond' first appeared in the anthology *A Clear Dawn: New Asian Voices from Aotearoa New Zealand*, Auckland University Press, 2021.

'a conversation' first appeared in *Starling*. This poem was read virtually by Louise Wallace for Paula Green's *Poetry Shelf* on National Poetry Day 2020.

'tell me' first appeared in *Starling*.

'tomorrow will be the same but not as this is' first appeared in the online archive *Stay Home Diary*, Bitter Melon Press, 2020. This poem also appeared in *Starling*.

'field notes on Lewis Hyde's *The Gift*' first appeared in *Starling*.

'night' first appeared in *Starling* as 'Lessons'.

Lily Holloway (born in 1998, she / they) is a queer writer and postgraduate English student. While she mostly writes poetry, she has also tried her hand at non-fiction, fiction and playwriting. You can find her work in places like *Starling*, *Midway Journal*, *Scum*, *The Pantograph Punch* and *The Spinoff* amongst various other literary nooks and crannies. In 2020 she was honoured to receive the Shimon Weinroth Prize in Poetry, the Kendrick Smithyman Scholarship in Poetry and second place in the Charles Brasch Young Writers' Essay Competition. In her spare time she enjoys op-shopping, letter writing, visiting small towns and collecting vintage Teletubbies paraphernalia. She is passionate about survivor advocacy and taking up space. You can find a list of her writing at lilyholloway.co.nz.

Tru Paraha resides in Tāmaki Makaurau in the suburb of Tukituki Muka (aka Herne Bay). She works as a choreographer and director, having enjoyed an extensive career in experimental dance, theatre and audio-visual arts. She is currently in the final year of a postdoctoral research fellowship in the English and Drama department at the University of Auckland. Moving between choreography, philosophy and creative writing, Tru produces live performances, artists' pages and poems drawing on materials from deep space. She is a member of the International Dark-Sky Association and advocate for the preservation of the night sky as a world cultural heritage.

Modi Deng is a pianist based in London, currently pursuing postgraduate performance studies on a scholarship at the Royal Academy of Music. Her Chinese name 默笛 means 'silent flute', which her father drew from a poem by Tagore. Performances with her ensemble, the Korimako Trio, have taken her throughout the UK and her concerts have been broadcast on *BBC Radio 3* and *RNZ Concert*. After growing up in Dunedin, she went on to complete a Master of Music with First Class Honours on a Marsden research scholarship, while completing a Bachelor of English at the University of Auckland. Modi cares deeply about literature (diaspora and poetry), music, psychology and her family.

First published 2021
Auckland University Press
University of Auckland
Private Bag 92019
Auckland 1142
New Zealand
www.aucklanduniversitypress.co.nz

© Lily Holloway, Tru Paraha, Modi Deng, 2021

ISBN 978 1 86940 945 6

A catalogue record for this book is available from the National Library of New Zealand

This book is copyright. Apart from fair dealing for the purpose of private study, research, criticism or review, as permitted under the Copyright Act, no part may be reproduced by any process without prior permission of the publisher. The moral rights of the authors have been asserted.

Design by Greg Simpson

Printed in Singapore by Markono Print Media Pte Ltd
This book was printed on FSC® certified paper

AUP new poets 8

Lily Holloway
Tru Paraha
Modi Deng

Edited and with a foreword by Anna Jackson

AUCKLAND UNIVERSITY PRESS